BOOK OF HATS

Book

of

Hats

Poems By Allen Cohen
Drawings By Ann Cohen

REGENT PRESS
Oakland, California

Second Edition

Poems ©2003 by Allen Cohen
Drawings ©2003 by Ann Cohen
Preface © 2003 by Gerald Nicosia

Acknowledgments:
The Jazz Musician was published in *Beatitude 2.*
The Boxer was published in *Oxygen* # 7

Library of Congress Cataloging-In-Publication Data

Cohen, Allen.
  Book of hats : poems / by Allen Cohen ; drawings by Ann Cohen.--
1st ed.
    p cm.
  ISBN 1-58790-062-9
    1. San Francisco (Calif.)--Poetry. 2 Secondhand trade--Poetry. 3.
Retail trade--Poetry. 4. Hat trade--Poetry. I. Cohen, Ann, 1947- II. Title.

PS3603.O33B66 2003
811'.6--dc22

                                                      2003067463

OTHER BOOKS BY ALLEN COHEN:

CHILDBIRTH IS ECSTASY w/photographs by Stephen Walzer
REAGAN POEMS
SAN FRANCISCO ORACLE FACSIMILE EDITION (Editor)
THE HAIGHT ASHBURY IN THE SIXTIES (CDROM)
AN EYE FOR AN EYE MAKES THE WHOLE WORLD BLIND:
POETS ON 9/11 (Editor w/Clive Matson)

Manufactured in the U.S.A.
REGENT PRESS
6020-A Adeline
Oakland, CA 94608

for Avrum Rubenstein (1918-1995)
  for his lifelong dedication
    to his art and ideals

Self Portrait   Avrum Rubenstein

CAST OF CHARACTERS

PREFACE

Allen Cohen knows North Beach—the Italians who lost their youth and sunny Mediterranean dreams, the has-been boxers and would-be cappuccino-slingers, the genuine eccentrics like the lady who flies her airplane naked inside a fur coat, the criminal sharpies, and the profoundly troubled ordinary folks whose costume—be it that of a go-go dancer or a tough-assed biker—is their only armor against a killing world. He sits behind his hat-clerk's desk and listens patiently to their banter—functioning as a kind of quiet Buddha mirror to help them see themselves, and perhaps to offer them a new helmet with which to return to the fray. These are poems of truest compassion for endlessly bedeviled humanity—rendered in the simplest, cleanest lines and the crisp bell tones of a tenor horn on K-JAZ coming out of an open doorway one magic evening on Grant Avenue.

Ann Cohen's illustrations—wacky, merry, offbeat—form a dizzying kaleidoscopic backdrop to the poems, making the poems seem to dance off the page in frenzied bursts of energy that contrast pleasantly with the gentle, steady voice of the poet-sage.

Gerald Nicosia

San Francisco

9

INTRODUCTION

The poems in the *Book of Hats* were written while I worked at the Shlock Shop on Grant Avenue in the North Beach district of San Francisco. Avrum Rubenstein, the owner of the Shlock Shop, was an artist who had been painting for forty years at *The Scene Gallery,* his storefront studio and gallery next door to the Shlock Shop. Avrum died in 1995, and the shop closed a few months later despite the best efforts of his children to keep it going. It was replaced by yet another trendy boutique. He employed only poets and artists to sell his large collections of old and new junk (shlock), and old and new hats.

Old Indian baskets, whale teeth, antique dentist tools, sock monkey dolls, political and labor buttons from the thirties, old beer cans, Eskimo knitting tools and hundreds of other old relics were clogged into the many glass cabinets and cases that lined the walls and floor space. Hats were everywhere — stacked on shelves, swinging on dummies' heads from the rafters and hanging on nails from the walls. The sound of jazz from KJAZ radio echoed through two inside speakers and one larger speaker above the front door facing Grant Avenue. It created the perfect background and beat for the passages through the shop's labyrinth.

Somehow in this era of fast food and franchises this old, dusty, dark fossil of a bygone era had survived. It provided a small wage plus commission on sales to the poets and artists working part time there. I was working four or five hour shifts sitting behind an old wood desk writing, reading and doing political mass mailings, and occasionally selling a hat or antiquity.

North Beach is a crossroads of the world where Italians and Chinese live and open restaurants, and artists and poets still talk and write in the old hotels, coffee houses and saloons. Topless bars and peepshows still draw in the lonely and the tourists. The rich from Telegraph Hill bear entreaties from the derelict, drunk and stoned, and sometimes move down the social ladder to Grant avenue, fried chicken legs and moldy hotel rooms.

These poems are based on transcriptions of interactions with people who came into the dark shadows of the Shlock Shop and left some part of their being there with me. I would recognize that magical moment of opening and begin writing, scribbling fast on the nearest envelope or flyer or paper bag, so as not to forget the nuances of the revelation of character that had just occurred. The poems reveal the humor and poignancy of the human person that we so often forget to notice in the techno-electro speed of contemporary life.

THE OLD MAN

An old Italian man
    about 65
wearing a shabby, small brimmed,
    grey fedora
hovers at the door on a hot day
    in North Beach.
He gazes longingly
    at the cool white Panama hats.
I invite him in. He tries on
    a short brimmed Panama.
He is remembering his youth
    on the Mediterranean
the white beaches, hot sun
    and dark bodies.
He asks the price.
    I tell him, "$25".
The sides of his mouth drop
    as he realizes
he can't afford a new cool,
    pure, white straw hat.
His youth slowly fades
    from his mind.
He whispers, "I'm sorry,"
    and returns to Grant avenue.

THE LOVERS

Today unusual thundershowers
    break the heat.

I'm on a slow night shift —
    a couple walks in arm in arm.

The tall man, mustachioed, in mid-thirties
    asks me if I would answer

an important question
    with the absolute truth.

"What's the question?" I ask.
    He looks at the woman.

She's in mid-twenties, tall, brightly beautiful,
    wearing a white ruffled blouse.

"Which one of us," he replies,
    "loves the other more?"

"To answer that," I say.
    "I will have to consult

my crystal ball, meditate a while
    and watch you very closely."

"Isn't she beautiful?" He asks.
    "Yes, very beautiful," I answer.

He is pressing against her from behind.
    "That feels so good," he says.

"It feels more wonderful to me," she responds.
    "Look at her eyes! Aren't they gorgeous?" He asks.

I look into her blue green eyes
    with brown flecks floating through the iris.

"Yes, they are beautiful," I say.

"What kind of hat," she asks,

would look good on me?"
    I try a Panama on her.

"No, winter's coming," she says abruptly.
    Then I put a Sam Spade hat on her head.

She allows me to place the wide brimmed hat
    on and tilt it rakishly.

"No, I don't like it. It's too large,"
    she says disappointedly.

He finds the last Roaring Twenties hat
    amongst the overhead rare hats

hanging from nails in the rafters and walls.
    It's a light gray fedora

with a black band that George Raft
    might have worn and she loves it.

I give him a brown felt Safari hat
    that makes him look like John Wayne.

"You look great!" They say to each other
    and kiss passionately.

The man pays $52.12 and I say,
    "Now I can answer your question.

"You both love each other equally,
    but if you don't, you're in big trouble."

She leans over and whispers loudly,
    "He has another woman!"

Standing at the door, he overhears and replies,
    "that's not true. I don't!"

They exit laughing onto Grant avenue.

TERRIBLE TERRY

On a warm slow Tuesday afternoon
I'm reading in John Updike's novel
The Coup that in an African village
everyone touches even teenage boys.
But in America once you're a teenager
in your own room, through adulthood
and middle age, there is so little touching,
until old age when we begin to return
to the void and doctors and nurses
touch and tear our helpless bodies
as if we were infants again

While reading, a red faced man enters.
He has a blond beard and tattoos
on his arms and chest.
He is wearing a blue shirt and jeans
that are slipping down his waist.
He asks if that's KJAZ on the radio.
"Can I listen a minute?"

He holds his side and twists his face in pain.
"Broken rib!" He remarks.
"Three rookie cops decided to practice on me.
They think they own the neighborhood.
I was born here. I was drunk.
They threw me in the drunk tank for seven hours."
He shows me black and blue marks on his arm.
"I told them a thing or two.
That's why they call me Terrible Terry.
What's your name?"

He thrusts a very strong muscular hand
toward me and I shake it firmly.
"I'm shipping out in a couple of weeks.
That's where I belong, at sea.
Six or seven months and I'll have
a pocketful of money. Then I can buy
a couple of your brass lighters,
and some new clothes and some toot.
Love that music! I'll be seein' ya."
He slowly returns to Grant avenue.

THE JAZZ MUSICIAN

Warm Tuesday evening,
    KJAZ on radio as usual.
A tall black man comes in
    with graying beard and no front teeth.
He is dressed in a long denim coat
    over a blue jump suit and Irish cap.
When I look at him, he says,
    "Every time I pass by the music draws me in."
Supersax with L.A. Singers
    are playing Star Eyes with ensemble sax breaks.
He closes his eyes and weaves
    his body around his own inner sun.
Then Miles Davis comes on
    playing My Funny Valentine.
"That's my man," he says.
    "I played guitar with Miles before McLaughlin."
He scat sings around the melody.
    "Yeah, I played around at the Jazz Workshop,
and the Both/And, but I never played the Blackhawk.
    I sat in with Bags and Jimmy Smith.
I'm playing piano and organ now.
    Got to keep growin' and giggin'."
He swings out onto Grant avenue.

THE SADOMASOCHISTS

A man in his late thirties
    wearing a baseball jacket enters.
        He is tall with a loping stride,
            round face and a pencil-thin mustache.

He is accompanied by a beautiful
    platinum blond woman
        with a deep, leisure tan
            and a tight tweed suit.

They look around gazing intently
    at the myriad glass cases and strange objects.
        The man swaggers over to me
            and surreptitiously whispers,

"Do you have any handcuffs?"
    The woman pokes him in the ribs.
        He adds, "Do you have any leather straps?"
        He is smirking now — she walks away.

I reply loudly, "leather straps?"
    He looks around nervously,
        "Shh! Not so loud.
        How about chains

or anything like that?"
    "No, I don't have straps
        or chains or anything like that!"
        He walks over to the woman

and slaps her sharply on the buttocks.
    She responds smilingly, "Noo!"
        He kisses her passionately, and rubbing
        her shoulders, they exit to Grant avenue.

THE BOUNCER

On a muggy Sunday
a short haired woman
in a brown raincoat
asks for a dark green beret
for her boyfriend.
Then she asks for
the bright green beret.
She looks at both.
"The dark green," she decides.
"He is too conservative
for the bright green."

She takes out a checkbook.
"We can't take checks without
a local check guarantee card."
She looks at me unbelievably.

I say, "Well, I'll trust you."

"Don't I know you?" She asks.
"Didn't we meet at the Toy Fair,
at Richard Erickson's booth?"

"Oh yes, I remember you." I answer.

"I always meet people
I know in North Beach," she continues.
"When I first moved here in 1980
I got a job as a bouncer
at a jazz club called Caudells.

I used to bounce all the drunk
North Beach poets and I got
to know them and the musicians."

"You were a bouncer?" I ask

"Yeah, It was easy.
The bartender had the brass knuckles
but he only had to use them once.

Even when I got a job
in an advertising agency,
I kept the bouncer's job.
I liked it so much, ten dollars a night
and all I could drink.

"A couple of years later
I went to a film festival
with one of the agency people
to see a Brazilian film.
But it was announced that
the film hadn't arrived
and there would be a showing
of the film of the Spoleto
International Poetry Festival instead.
It was in memoriam for the Italian
film maker Passolini who had just died."

"Yes, he was a good poet too," I added.

"But the poets," she continued,
were all speaking in their own languages,
German, French, Austrian, whatever.
My friend wanted to leave
but I wanted to wait for
the American and English poets.
Then there's a long shot
of the stage from the hillside
and the camera zooms in
and there's all the poets
I bounced from Caudells
in North Beach and I yell out,
'I know those guys
I bounced them from Caudells",
and my friend looked at me.
She thought I was nuts.
Well, thanks. Have a good weekend!"

She walks as quick
as she talks out to Grant avenue.

THE COLLECTOR

A bearded beer bellied Hispanic man
wearing a Pumping Iron T-shirt
looks at WW II pilot's helmets
and other old hats and says,
"I collect hats for twenty years, now.
People think I'm nuts.
But I love them — porcelain dolls too
and my wife collects Chinese dolls.
They're worth a lot now.
I used to go to the Ozarks
and get old stuff there
but five or six years ago
somebody went up and told them.
You can't get the time of day there now.
Funny how people collect old stuff.
I got old oil paintings and old frames.
I got a two hundred year old French frame.
I don't want to sell them.
I just go into my room where
they're all lined up and I sit
in an old stuffed chair and I relax.
Feel right at home there;
feel right at home.

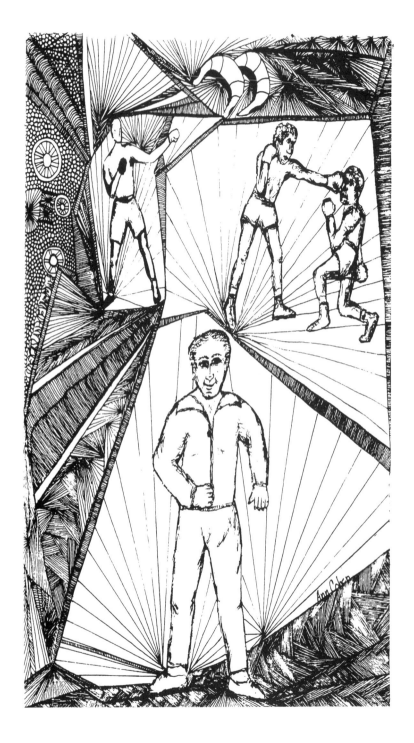

THE BOXER

A short, lean,
gray haired man
about sixty flashes
a sweet smile
as he enters
one late afternoon.
He is wearing
a blue warm-up jacket.
He looks at
the English Bobby helmet
hanging from the ceiling
and mentions that
he should have bought
a couple of the old
Bobby helmets in London
when they changed
helmets three years ago.

"I come to Frisco
every three years.
Go to City Lights
and the Cafe Trieste
and think that
I'm talking with
all the new artists
and writers.
I was here in the Fifties —
Allen and Jack and me
started it all —
I'm only kidding!

I'm just an old boxer
from Milwaukee.
You can tell a boxer
from the way he walks.
I came to meet Ron Lundee
in Redwood City in a hotel.
He was Light Heavyweight Champ
in 1937 and he's 71 now.

So I was sitting
in the lobby
watching people
walk to the desk.
But when he came in
I knew it was Ron.
He had this balance
like a ball bearing
was inside him
and this cockiness in his walk.
See, there's two things
you never know
about a fighter
when he comes
into the ring -
his punch
and his heart.
You see a guy
with rippling muscles.
You don't know
if he's got a punch.
The punch comes
from the right foot,
right from the sole
of the right foot.
You can feel it
come through, whoosh!
I always tell a boxer
to take his natural stance
— nothing special —
however he
feels comfortable,
that's him!

Before a fight
the boxer weighs in at noon.
What do you think
a fighter eats then?
Not steak, it's too dry.
A fighter has to sweat,
so he has to eat

something greasy
like pancakes or waffles.
A good fighter
has to sweat. Be shining
with sweat in the ring.
If he don't sweat,
he's gonna wilt."

I show him
an old leather
boxer's helmet
on a dummy's head
hanging from the ceiling.
He remarks, "I don't like
my boxers to wear helmets.
It makes them feel safe
and takes away
their peripheral vision.
I'm going over
to City Lights and buy
Coney Island of the Mind.
I lost my copy.
I like Ferlinghetti
better than Ginsberg.
His language is leaner.
See ya!"
He walks cockily
on to Grant Ave.

THE TOPLESS DANCER

A young woman wearing shorts
and a large straw hat with
a bouquet of silk in front
and feathers pointing back
enters briskly on a warm day.
She has a bare midriff, long legs
and a thin shapely body.

She says, "You must be Mr. Shlock."
I say, "nice hat you have on."
"I wear it on stage too," she responds.
"Do you dance?" I ask.

"I dance at the Mitchell Brothers.
Oh! You're incense is only 35 cents.
Do you have Gardenia? A man
gave me a bottle of Gardenia perfume.
I wear it all the time."

"Are the police going to shut them down?" I ask.

"No they can't touch them ....
Listen, all I do is dance.
Then I sit on a man's lap,
put my arms around him,
ask him if he wants company
and talk to him. Then usually
he gives me 10 bucks.
They aren't allowed to touch me.
It's no more then you might do
walkin' with your sweetie down Grant avenue.
You should get Gardenia incense."

She buys lotus instead and asks
if I think she's cheap
because she's just buying incense.
"No, I don't think your cheap," I answer.
"Then you must be starin' at my bare cleavage."
"Yes, I am," I admit with a laugh.
"Have a good day, Mr. Shlock."

JOE'S PLACE

A young man about 25 comes in
and asks to see the pilot's helmets.
He is wearing a T-shirt with a picture
of a wood frame building and the words
JOE'S CAFE - NORTHAMPTON, MASS. on it.
"Joe's Cafe must be famous in Northhampton?" I ask
"Oh yes! Very famous," he says.

"I remember driving through Kansas,"
I recollect, "just out of college in 1962.
There was a sign on the side
of the road saying, JOE'S PLACE
and 100 yards further another sign, JOE'S PLACE,
and then another, and then, JOE'S PLACE 1/4 MILE
and finally, TURN HERE FOR JOE'S PLACE.
Who could resist? We took the exit
for Joe's Place. Soon we arrived
at a large, brick ranch style building.
We walked in the door and came face to face
with a 24 x 10 foot mural replica
of Leonardo da Vinci's Last Supper.

"On the wall to the left
there is a large portrait of a man
with a thick mustache standing
behind a cash register with pride.
'Who painted that Last Supper?'
I asked the man showing us to a table.

'I did,' he says. 'I studied art in Italy
and found descriptions of how
the Last Supper looked when
it was first painted in the 15th century.
Now many of the details have faded.
When I returned, I painted the mural
with the details that are no longer
visible in the original painting.
And that painting,' "he points

at the portrait with cash register,"
'is my father, Joe. He started this place;
ran it for 25 years and sent me to Italy.
He died three years ago.
I run the restaurant now.'
"We had a great lunch at Joe's Place."

The young man with the Joe's Cafe T-shirt
liked the fur lined pilot's helmet
but couldn't afford the $40 to buy it.

THE MUSIC LOVER

It's a cold but sunny Monday.
A short, gray haired woman enters
wearing a short sleeve blouse.
cigarette is dangling from her mouth.

"I love your music," she says.
"How do you get such a clear sound?
Music is so loud these days.
Millions of dollars of equipment
and it sounds like a thunderstorm.
Do you remember the '40s?
Frank Sinatra used to sing
with Tommy Dorsey
using three microphones.
You could hear everything
clear as a bell.
For twenty years my ears
have been deafened.

"I've been here dozens of times.
I just like to hear
a few bars of music.
I know what you got.
I don't want to buy anything.
I don't need a hat.
Such pretty music,
good-bye!"
She returns to the cold street.

THE PORK PIE HAT

It's a cool, quiet May evening.
The music on KJAZ is slow ballads.
I'm reading about how the military
can't catch drug smugglers
when a young round bodied, round faced
guy with round horn rimmed glasses
comes bouncing through the door.
He is wearing a sweat shirt
and a grey Pork Pie hat.
It's the kind we used to carry
with such a low crown
that it wouldn't fit on the head
without breaking the pork pie shape.
Some people bought them anyway
because they looked like the Pork Pies
of the Forties and Fifties that
Lester Young and other jazz musicians wore.

I ask the young man how he got
the hat to stay on his head and
he shows me what he had done.
He gently and evenly punches up
the center of the crown just enough
to fit on the brow and still keep
the crease around the edge
that forms the pork pie.
He has also bent up the front
and back of the brim making it
look like Hunt Hall's hat from
the East Side Kids of the Fifties.
"Where did you get the hat," I ask.

"I got it from a woman
I know in New York," he begins,
for moving her futon across town.
She got it from a guy who she was dating
because she loved this hat.
Then she ditched him and kept the hat.
You know those clubs in New York
where the doorman chooses
the people who can come in
from the crowd at the door.
They pick the hippest lookin' people.
Well, when they see this hat,
they say, 'hey, you with the hat
come on in.' Every time, I get right in.
They call it a Home Boy hat in New York."
He puts the Pork Pie back on
and bounces back onto Grant Avenue.

Ann Cohen © Oct 1971

THE PILOT

On a cool, sunny February day
a woman dressed in blue
with strings of glass beads
around her neck bounces in.
She is slightly inebriated
and is accompanied by
a quiet bearded man
wearing a dark blue blazer.

"How much are those pilot helmets
in the window," she asks.

"$35," I answer and place
the helmets on the counter.
"I have Spanish WWII helmets
in black and brown, and this
cloth English training helmet
from 1938 or 39, and this
contemporary one that fits all sizes"

She tries them on explaining,
"I'm learning to fly a Cessna
wearing a mink coat and a helmet
with nothing on underneath."

"Well, I guess it's cold up there,"
I remark smilingly.

"We're doing it from Boston, "
she continues. "I like it there now.
I used to be a hippy but hippies
all got rich and became yuppies.

"Not me," I say. "I used to edit
the San Francisco Oracle in the Haight."

Undaunted she says, "I was one of the first
street artists. I lived on Cole Street
and went to graduate school with Carol Doda.
I just took my husband into
the Condor and the Garden of Eden.
They just don't do that in Boston.

Has San Francisco really changed?"

"Yes, it has," I answer. "There's been
downtown development and the Gay culture
and Aids and Diane Feinstein."

"Well, they still got naked girls and Chinatown.
It can't have changed too much.
I've got four people looking
for this helmet. But I want it in red."

"They don't make it in red."

"Well, I'll paint a red rose on it,
she responds. "My husband
just bought me a full length black mink.
Do you take American Express?"

"No, Master or Visa."

"That's good. I can't find
my American Express anyway.
You know, all that an accountant
is good for is to find your checkbook
and mine doesn't even do that.
Well, I'll get this new brown helmet,
and I'll think about you
as I fly over Boston
in my mink and pilot's helmet.
Bye, dearie."

She spreads her arms
and flies onto Grant avenue.

THE TV PRODUCER

It's Monday, the day after the Superbowl.
There's a snappy chill in the air.
An ABC-TV assistant producer enters.
He had come in for a hat
during the Democratic convention
and now he's back in San Francisco
to shoot the Superbowl.
He is short and round, smokes cigars
and is wearing a black warm-up jacket
with an ABC logo on it.

"I was setting up some shots
at the Superbowl," he says.
"I sent a crew to interview
you during the convention
but you weren't in."

"I was probably lobbying at Moscone
for the Peace and Environmental Coalition,"
I answer with some disappointment.

Pointing at me he says to his brother
who he is showing around North Beach,
"He is one of the few pure ones left.
I sold my ass in 1976.
You don't know how fucked it is -
They had eight cameras
on Reagan tossing the kickoff coin.
He's falling asleep at press conferences."

"Why don't you guys in the press
let the public know what a con it is?"
"Me!" He says. "I'm just a piece of fuzz
on the bottom of a pawn
on a giant chessboard."

"Well, what else do you hear?
Do you think he'll invade Nicaragua?"
"Not Nicaragua," he answers.
"He wants Cuba. Cuba in the spring.

They've been digging tunnels
from Guantanamo into Cuban territory
to prepare for an attack.
They'll knock out Cuba in a few weeks."

"Is that what you hear in Washington?" I ask.
"No, that's the word in New York."
He shakes my hand and he and his brother
return to TV land.

THE SINNER

It's a cool Sunday,
first day of March.
Sun is alternating with clouds.
A young man in his late twenties enters.
He is thin, about six foot tall,
well dressed with suit and tie.
Looking at me timidly he asks,
"Do you think two people can be
in perfect telepathic communication,
so that the other person is in your mind?"

"No, I don't," I answer.
It's probably your imagination."

He shuffles his feet a little,
bites his lip and shyly says,
"I'd like to ask you
one more question,
if you don't mind?"

"Go ahead," I say
though I'm sure my forehead
has ten creases in it
and my eyes are squinting.

"Do you think," he continues,
"that a man who goes out
with a lot of women is sinful,
has committed sinful acts?"

"I don't believe in sin," I answer.
"We sometimes make mistakes though."

"Thanks," he says with
his chin against his chest.
He turns quickly
and disappears.

ZORRO

A man wearing old, brown
    leather jacket, pants
        slipping down his legs,

teeth missing from his mouth,
    one of the mad wraiths
        who haunt North Beach

asks me for a Zorro hat.
    I give him black, flat crown,
        wide brim Flamenco dancer hat.

He smiles toothlessly and says,
    "That's it!" He tries it on,
        tilts it and looks into the mirror.

"You think I can do it, man.
    You think I can be Zorro."
        "You can be whoever you want," I answer.

"Zorro's my hero, man
    like Jesus is yours."
        "No, I am my own hero," I say.

"I got to get the rest of it —
    black on black and some steel."
        He pretends to whip out a sword.

"You think I can do it, man?
    Am I Zorro?"
        "Go for it, if you want."

"Will you hold it for me, man.
    I'll be back before Halloween.
        I'll be back."

THE TALKER

It's a warm summer day.
A few tourists take
a turn around the counters
but don't buy anything.
Then a man about 35
with thick glasses enters.
He is wearing a dress shirt
and tie with his jacket,
thrown over his shoulder.
He is eating an Italian pastry,
but abruptly asks me
if I like coffee houses.
I laugh and ask him why he asks.

"Do you think it would be nice
to work at the Cafe Trieste?
I just got a job there.
I think I'll like it.
I always wanted to work
in a coffee house.
I used to be in retail management
but I've always dreamed,
even as a kid,
of working in a coffee house.

"I worked for Best and Company.
But always in these big chains,
they make decisions at the top
and when you no longer fit, you're gone.
I get seriously depressed
when I don't work.

"Luckily my wife wants me
to do what I want. To start over,
even if I have to start
one step back,
then go forward.
At least I'll be fulfilling my dream.

"My wife is getting worried.
but tonight I"ll be able
to pick her up from work,
and smile and tell her
I got a job at my first
interview with the Cafe Trieste.
I always do well at interviews.

"My last job was selling wine
for a small winery distributor.
He picked me from two hundred applicants.
But I didn't like the product very much,
and it's so competitive in wines.
But I always loved coffee.
Maybe some day I'll own
my own coffee house.
I'd have musical instruments
hanging from the ceilings
and music sheets on the walls.
But I know I should just
learn the business first.
Do you like your work?"

"Yes, I do a lot of reading
and writing while working."

"I would be bored," he continues.
"I like people.
I'm sort of natural with people.
My counsellor says
I'm such a good talker
I could wake the dead.
But I've got to do something
or else I get out of control,
very depressed. Do you think
it's alright working
for a few dollars an hour
at a coffee house?"

"If that's what you want, sure,"
I respond. "We are all haunted
by this idea of success and failure.
If you're not Brooks Shield

or Sylvester Stallone,
you're nothing. If you
don't earn fifty thou
you're a failure, and then
when they take it away
or you lose it,
you've lost everything.
But real values aren't material."

"Yeah," he begins again,
I know what you mean.
I am always thinking about myself.
How I'm going to get another job?
What value do I have,
if I'm not making bucks?
But what can you do?"

"I try to think about
helping humanity, doing
something for other people," I answer.
"You can't be a failure
if you're serving food
at St. Anthony's or
making phone calls for the Freeze."

"You mean," he says,
"I won't be depressed anymore
if I help other people.
I've never done that.
I just get depressed
and always think about myself.
That's a good idea.
It'll be hard.
Just volunteer to help others.
Thanks, nice meeting you.
That's a good idea!
He wanders in mid-sentence
out to Grant avenue.

THE BIKER

It's a warm Indian summer day.
A tall, goateed biker comes in
wearing a Harley T-shirt and spiked belt
with knife and chains hanging from it.
He walks around looking intently in all
the showcases, and returns to the front desk.
He leans forward and says, "Others
have probably told you this, but this
isn't a store, it's a museum."

I notice a recently stitched scar
about 3 inches long on his cheek.
"That's pretty nasty! How'd you get it."

"Well, Friday night I was jammin'
with my band, the Ding Dong Daddies,
finally, I got a hot band, don't
have to teach them nothin', we can play
anythin' — blues, hot rock, anythin' —
when Little Brother, my sidekick, hit me
with a saw! Just came at me for no reason.
He's got a lot of pressure and he's usin'
amphetamine. That don't help.
It takes the gentle out of you.
He comes at my head first."

He leans his head forward revealing
a six inch scar on his shaved crown.
"Then he comes at my face. I grab his arm
and twist it. I hear it break. I lost
three pints of blood. I say to him,
'What you doin' brother?
You fuckin' me up! You killin' me!'

"He tells me, 'I'm sorry. I fucked up.
I didn't know what I was doin'.
I gotta get help.'

"I don't know what to do. I don't
want to hurt him no more. I'd just
put him away and then he'd hate me.

I'd be in jail and his wife and kid
will hate me. It's those amphetamines,
they take the gentle out of you.
Maybe if he gets help? He's like
my little brother and he turns on me.
We were jammin', havin' a great old time,
till he hit me with that saw.
Best band I've ever had!"

"Maybe," I say, "you can forgive this one."
"Yeah, I won't forget, but I'm
gonna have to forgive. I don't
wanna put him away. I really don't.
Well, my names Mike."
"I'm Allen."
"So long, Al."
He strides out to the sunlit street.

THE RED FACED MAN

It's a slow sunny July day.
I've sold only one Irish tweed cap.
A red faced man, sweating,
with a large pot belly comes in.
He is holding a framed 3 dimensional
picture of Calzone's Pizzeria.
It is part painting and free standing
cut-out construction of people
sitting inside the restaurant
and walking outside on Columbus Avenue.
"I know you don't want one
made for your store," he says.
"You made it?" I ask.
"Yes, me and my partner,
but he had a nervous breakdown.
You can't desert someone like that.
But I'm getting nervous too.
I stopped smoking and now
I'm putting on weight.
If I had a new lover,
I'd probably eat the vaseline
before I had a chance to use it."

"How much is the painting?" I ask.
"Oh, $330 with the frame.
I know you don't want it,
but I like to make people smile.
Since I stopped smoking,
my nose and throat are always stuffed."
"Why don't you try acupuncture?
That might help," I suggest.

"You know I just turned sixty," he continues.
"It's scary. I think I"d rather gain 60 pounds
or lose $600 than turn 60."
I smile maybe giggle at his remark.
"Well, thanks for laughing."
He hurries into the hot sun.

THE MAN ABOUT TOWN

It's a slow, cloudy November day.
A tall elegantly dressed man
in his mid-thirties stumbles in
and lets out a drunken, windy sigh.
"Welcome, you must have journeyed far
but you've finally arrived in hat heaven."

"You're damn right! I've come from
three days in a Las Vegas jail.
Your sign says, 'NO FOOD, DOGS,
DRUNKS OR PLEASES'. I'm one of those.
I think I'm a please. I just came
from the Mabuhay. It's boring.
Everything's boring. I've got just
two problems — redheaded women
and chocolate chip cookies."

"It don't look like the cookies
are harming you're waistline," I comment wryly.
"I like to spread them all over
my and anyone else's body," he says.
I've fucked every woman in San Francisco."

"Not true, you don't even know my lover," I reply.
He smiles slyly and looks at his watch.
"Don't tell me you got a date
with her in ten minutes?"
He smiles again and then tightens his lips
and hits one of the showcases with his fist.

"They arrested me when I stepped
off the plane in Las Vegas.
Somebody must have told them I was coming.
But I showed those bastards,
I just stared at them. For three days
I stared at them. I didn't blink.
They didn't know what they had on their hands.
They had to let me out.
I challenged the guard to an arm wrestling match.
I told him if I win, you let me out.

He was a weight lifter with big muscular arms.
And look at me! I'm a scarecrow, right?
Well, I just concentrate my Chi power -
we join hands and whoosh!
I put him right down and he let's me out.
Then I go into a casino,
walk right up to a roulette table
and put my last $5 down and
my number comes up three times in a row.
Then I go to the track
and put $50 on a horse that pays $40.
Then I get on a plane and come back.
I'm a tough guy. You can't tell
because of the way I'm dressed.
But you should see me in my torn jacket
with the buckles and medals
Let me try a hat! A nice one
I can crush and put in my jacket."

I give him a soft, gray, wool felt fedora
with a black band that looks classy
but is really cheap with a short life.
He tries it on, looks in the mirror
and asks its price.
"$28," I reply
"Well, I'll come back for it," he says
and heads for the door.
"Why did they bust you in Vegas?" I ask.
"Because I'm so tall and handsome," he answers
and stumbles out into the approaching night.

THE DOLLAR

It's a warm Sunday afternoon.
    An old man with a grey Lincoln beard
        and a dark toothless mouth enters.

When he speaks, he leans over
    from the waist shooting
        his words at me.

He is wearing a cap
    that says, Italian Athletic Club.
        He notices the row of Panama hats.

"Up here on Union street, years ago," he begins,
    "they used to block Panamas.
        Place called Panama Hatties. Know that?

"I got a dollar to spend
    I wanna buy something for a dollar."
        He walks around looking in every cabinet and case.

I try English riding caps and top hats
    on two young women. One says,
        "I need a cap like this

because I'm wearing this guy's Stetson cap
    but I just gotta get rid of him.
        I know he's gonna take his cap with him."

The old man comes around to the front again.
    "What do you got for a dollar?" he asks loudly
        I show him old lucky poker chips

with embossed images of horses, elephants and owls.
    "Do you have any cards from Las Vegas?"
        "No, I'm sorry I don't."

He puts his dollar on the counter
    and says, "I gotta get outta here."
        and scurries out to Grant avenue.

57

THE TRUCKER

It's Columbus day in North Beach—
parades, cappuccino, pasta.
Tourists walking up Grant Avenue.
A short round man wearing
a blue shirt enters.
He has a tan, thin lips,
and a tough but open face.

"I'm goin' to school to learn
to drive an 18 wheeler," he explains.
"What do you got that other drivers
won't laugh at at truck stops?
I used to drive a taxi
but truck driven's more money,
and you get to travel
the whole country, see places
besides San Francisco.
You go to school for $1500
and you get jobs as an independent.
Since they deregulated, there's jobs
and you're your own boss.
On the road nobody's lookin'
over your shoulder tellin' you
to do this and do that.
Then you can buy your own truck
and then two or three
and you're in business.
Everythin' is touched by a truck,
everythin' you got here.
But you gotta like bein' alone
on the road with nothin'
but your own thoughts."

While he's talking, I hand him
tweed Irish riding caps to try on.
He looks in the mirror
tilting and bending them.
He gives me a $20 bill to hold,
while he walks outside
to show the hat to his wife.
He returns with a blue

aerated, adjustable
California Highway Patrol cap on.
"You ought to carry this hat,"
he continues. "My wife thinks
the other drivers would make fun
of this Irish cap.
This Highway Patrol cap
will get you through the scales."

"The owner," I reply,
"doesn't like to carry caps,
just traditional and collectable hats."

"Well," he responds,
"maybe I'll pick up
the Irish cap in the winter
when it rains. See you
in a couple of months."
He trucks out to Grant avenue.

GUN COLLECTOR

It's a sunny, warm day.
I sit in the cool shade
listening to jazz and reading
about President Zia of Pakistan
deciding that democracy
and political parties are unIslamic.
A large 6 foot 4 inch man
in mid-twenties comes in,
looks around and asks me
what the shot gun shell is
that he sees in the front case.
I tell him it's a cigarette lighter
in a shell from WWII.

"Are antiques a good business
in San Francisco," he asks.
"I don't know," I answer.
"We just have small odd things
like whales teeth and fountain pens,
not old furniture and oak desks."

"I go to auctions in Connecticut a lot,"
he continues. "I collect old guns."

"All I've got," I reply pointing to them,
"is a couple of old toy rifles
and a theatrical 19th century
broadsword from Spain."
He looks at the sword.

"My friend," he responds, "has one
like this from the 17th century
and he paid only 35 dollars for it.
He appraises my stuff.
He's been collecting guns

since he was a kid.
His house and closets
are full of guns.
He's even got an anti-tank gun
in his basement, but he says
he can't find shells for it.
But I bet he's got some
shells stashed away.
He recently started counting
the ammo he's collected.
But when he reached
15 thousand rounds, he stopped.
He says if they ever outlaw
hand guns in Connecticut,
he'd take a backhoe and bury
everything he's got.
He'd never give it up.
Hey, so long!" He walks
out into the glaring sun.

THE ANGRY POET

A young man with a red beard,
  big barrel belly
    and a small back pack

asks for a cool hat he can wear
  on a train ride to New York.
    Something that will absorb sweat

and he can put tickets in.
  I show him a few hats
    but he thinks only a baseball cap will do.

"What are you going to do in New York?" I ask.
  "I'm doing some poetry readings
    in New York and Princeton," he answers.

"How did you get that set up?" I ask curiously.
  "My wife teaches at Princeton
    and my friend is an agent.

"My first book is being published
  by Black Bear Press in Mendocino."
    He shows me the galleys

of *Rome On The Highways*,
  a small book of prose poems
    that are strong, angry

staccato, one breath explosions
  on the fall of America.
    "I started writing," he continues,

"when I was laid off from the line
  at the Cadillac plant in Patterson, New Jersey.
    See, when you work on the line

"everything's repetitive and boring.
  So to keep from going nuts,
    I used to remember everything

"from my childhood with all the detail.

I could picture it in my mind.
        When I got laid off,

"I didn't know what to do with myself.
    So my wife told me to start writing
        all those pictures in my head,

"and I just kept doing it
    with those jazz beats
        and rhythms of the line."

I read him one of my calmer
    observational lyrics and he asks me
        to have coffee with him.

"I have to stay here
    and sell hats now, but
        how about tonight at six?" I ask.

"No, I've got to catch my train
    to New York at five. I'll see you."
        He swings out to Grant Avenue.

TRAVELER

I'm on a Tuesday night shift
sitting behind the desk and reading
about Cortez and Moctezuma,
when a slight man enters.
He is wearing a blue blazer
and has an aging but childlike face.
He asks for a beaver hat
that he can wear hiking in the Cascades,
a hat that will withstand rain and wear.
I show him a few old beavers
hanging from nails on the wall,
and the new fur felts
made of mostly rabbit hair,
and the suede Australian Bulldog hats.
They are all too expensive
and not quite the right fit.

"I wore a beaver hat
and went through two pairs of boots,
when I walked the Pacific Coast Trail
from Canada to Mexico, 2600 miles,
more than half of them alone.
A few years ago I bicycled
round the whole coast of Africa
except the Sudan because
there were no roads there."

"That's quite a feat!
You must have had some wild experiences."

"Well, frankly it was boring and repetitious,
but occasionally exciting and adventurous.
I ended up in Paris and slept
at Shakespeare and Company
My window overlooked Notre Dame.
If you're an author, you can
still sleep there for free.
They wanted me to run the bookstore
six months out of the year,
but there was no gain in it for me.
After all we do get older and
you can't just survive anymore."

He chooses a canvas Safari hat
that is durable and cheaper
and pays with a Visa card.

"When I entered the Sudan,
a border guard asked me
what my credit card was.
I explained what you could get
and do with it, and the guard said,
'But it is only plastic.' And so it is."

The young man
with his new beige Safari hat
and blue blazer walked out
toward a two week hike
through the Cascades.

WORLD WAR II VETERAN

An old man in his seventies,
    shock of white hair and a puckish smile,
      walking with an ivory handled cane

strolls in early on a warm Sunday.
    "Quiet day on the street," he says.
      "They just raised my prescription $10

"from 20 to 30 bucks in one month.
    These pharmacists don't know nothin'.
      I used to mix drugs in the thirties.

"You just needed a license like barbers.
    Morphine and cocaine were legal by script.
      There were no pimps either. Older girls

"used to take care of younger girls.
    There were yacht parties where
      we'd smoke morphine and cocaine.

"Yeah, these pharmacists can't even make aspirin.
    If there was a catastrophe
      they'd be outta drugs in a minute,

" 'cause they can't mix anything anymore.
    You know how much codeine costs to make?
      A penny and a half, same with all these drugs.

"Shit! Mechanics are the same way.
    I got a complete set of tools
      and I carry new breaks and an axle

"when I travel and I can put
    them on in an hour.
      All mechanics can do is charge a lot of money.

"In the war I could go into
    a hot boiler and fix it.
      I could pick up a burning frying pan

"and throw it out the porthole.
   I used to be 215 pounds
      but my stomach collapsed.

"I got a hernia and poisons in my stomach.
   They can't operate 'cause
      the poisons would spread.

"Yeah, Admiral Halsey knew who I was.
   I got the tough jobs on New Guinea.
   I was wounded and burned.

"I got new knees
   and my feet break out all the time.
      I won't let them operate anymore.

"I just go in for a check-up.
   See if the plumbing's working.
      Even during the war,

"they couldn't take care of everyone.
   One guy came from Europe to the Pacific
      all bandaged up ready to go into it again.

"I went back and I'd do it again, too.
   So long! Hot day! Take it easy!"
      He limps out onto Grant Avenue.

ALLEN COHEN BIOGRAPHY

Allen Cohen was born in Brooklyn, New York in 1940. Moving to San Francisco in the early 60s, he founded and edited the legendary *San Francisco Oracle*, the psychedelic, rainbow hued underground newspaper published in the Haight-Ashbury. He also helped originate rites of passage like the *Human-Be-In* in the Haight. He has published two books of poetry, *Childbirth Is Ecstasy* and *The Reagan Poems*. In 1991 he worked with Regent Press in Oakland, Ca. to publish a commemorative *Facsimile Edition* of the complete *San Francisco Oracle* in order to preserve it for posterity.

Since the early 80s he has been presenting his multi-image slide show *The Rise and Fall of the Haight-Ashbury in the 60s* in theaters and universities. In 1995 he authored a CD-ROM, *The Haight Ashbury in the 60s*. He has performed his poetry at music concerts, colleges, museums and coffeehouses.

Now he is working on a political book that takes a shot at reconstructing American politics. In 2001 he consulted with the San Diego Museum of Art on *High Societies* a sixties rock poster show, and produced a symposium on the Sixties for the show. In 2001 he edited *Peace News*, an emergency newspaper exploring alternatives to war. In 2002 he edited (with Clive Matson) *An Eye For An Eye Makes The Whole World Blind: Poets on 9/11* which won the 2003 PEN Oakland Josephine Miles Award for outstanding writing.

ANN COHEN

Ann Cohen was born in LA in 1947, and has lived in Walnut Creek, Ca. for the last 23 years. She has been teaching art and music in Walnut Creek elementary schools and her own in-home preschool since 1980. She has produced art and music events for children in Walnut Creek, and is a composer of children's songs. She has been active in her local arts community designing wigs for the Regional Arts Center in Walnut Creek for 20 years. She has been playing standup bass accompanying Allen Cohen's poetry since 1987, and has been performing her original environmental-folk music around the Bay Area. Her art is in many private collections and has appeared in *Beatitude* magazine, *Relix* magazine and Split Shift.